HOW TO SAY WHAT YOU MEAN, MEAN WHAT YOU SAY, AND GET WHAT YOU WANT

by Hena Khan

SCHOLASTIC INC.

New York Toronto London Auckland Sydney

Mexico City New Delhi Hong Kong Buenos Aires

ISBN: 0-439-57904-X

Design: Julie Mullarkey Gnoy
Illustrations: Kelly Kennedy

Copyright © 2004 by Scholastic Inc.

All rights reserved. Published by Scholastic Inc.

SCHOLASTIC, HOW TO SURVIVE ANYTHING, and associated logos are
trademarks and/or registered trademarks of Scholastic Inc.

12 11 10 9 8 7 6 5 4 3 2 1   4 5 6 7 8 9/C

Printed in the U.S.A.

First Scholastic printing, May 2004

CONTENTS

How to Survive This Book

Have you ever wished that you could:

- Hear a "yes" when you ask your folks to give you a raise in your allowance, or for permission to stay up late and watch your favorite TV show?

- Have the perfect line to say when you've been given a gift that you don't want or like?

- Know what to say to an adult who pushes you around or treats you like a kid—without getting detention, or being grounded?

- Make a bunch of new friends at a party where you don't know anyone—instead of standing alone in the corner and looking for the nearest exit?

- Stand up on the spot and give a speech without looking nervous, hyperventilating, or sweating so much you start creating a puddle?

Well, you can either go through life *wishing* for these things (and everything else you want), or you can find out how to get them. If you're ready to *get them*, then you've come to the right place!

This book is all about how to deal with other people and **get what you want** from them, whether it's a new bike, a fair deal, or a little respect. You'll also learn how to express yourself, get your message across, and make yourself understood so that you can get through to anyone!

So what do you need to get started? Just your head, and what comes in it—your brain and, of course, your tongue! That's because **the secret to getting what you want is often simply knowing what to say (and what not to say!), and how and when to say it.** You'll also learn how to **mean what you say**, and **say what you mean**. Which means that, by the end of this book, you'll know how to:

- Tell someone she's acting like an idiot (and be thanked for it!).

- Ask someone for the money he's owed you for six months that you were about to give up on.

- Say "no" to people who won't take no for an answer.
- Start a great conversation with that new kid in your gym class.
- Get through awkward moments when your tongue used to freeze in your mouth and you couldn't think of the right words to say.

Sounds like something you want? Then what are you waiting for? You can read this book from cover to cover, or you can start with a topic and flip around from there. Either way, it's all about getting what you want out of it!

Play the Game

To accompany *How to Get What You Want*, you've also got **Dots and Boxes**, a **fun-filled game of strategy and smarts.** It'll come in handy when you're ready to put your new "winning" skills to use.

The idea is to build boxes with the wall pieces so that you form as many squares as you can. The person who makes the final wall to create each square places his color dot inside and wins the box. Sounds simple? Well, it may seem that way. But, in reality, the game requires careful strategy to win—like figuring out how to outsmart your opponent by setting a trap (even if that initially means giving up a square or two). All this in a game about walls, dots, and boxes!

Just like in life, sometimes the simplest situations can prove to be the biggest challenges and your biggest opponent can be you, when you don't know what to do! **You'll get the hang of the game once you read through the survival tips and rules and play a few times.** So, grab another player and go for it!

Before jumping into the rest of the book, find out how good (or not) you already are at getting what you want, meaning what you say, and saying what you mean!

1. You've just gotten a brand new basketball and you're shooting some hoops when it starts to deflate. You try pumping it up again, but it's definitely busted. Do you:

   a. put it back in the box, wrap it up real nice, and give it to your little sis as an early birthday present.

   b. toss it in the trash, curse your bad luck, and start saving up for another.

   c. take it back to the store and make a case for having it fixed or replaced.

2. You're at your cousin's party where you don't know anybody. You're standing alone, feeling like a loser. Do you:

   a. make up a bunch of stuff about yourself to impress everyone.

   b. sneak into the kitchen, call your dad, and ask him to pick you up early.

   c. walk up to somebody, introduce yourself, and try to get a conversation going.

3. Your older sis is driving you nuts. Every time you want something, it's a battle—and you always lose! Do you:

   a. get your revenge by trashing her room when she's not home.

   b. try to convince your folks to send her away to boarding school.

   c. get her to work out some rules with you so things are fair.

4. You wish your math teacher would like you more, but it seems that she's already got her favorites—and you're not one of them! Do you:

   a. buy her a gift, write a poem about fractions, and offer to walk her dog for free.

   b. compliment her outfit and hair every day.

   c. act like you care about her class, try to follow the rules, and hope that does the trick.

5. All your friends are allowed to go on sleepovers, but your folks won't let you spend the night and always pick you up early. You're sick of being treated like a baby. Do you:

   a. plan to sneak out of the house the next time, before your parents even have the chance to say 'no'.

   b. yell at your folks and say that all of your friends get to do it, and that it's NOT FAIR that you can't!!

   c. brainstorm all of the reasons why you're mature enough for a sleepover and try to convince your folks.

6. You got a pair of kiddie roller skates that are three sizes too small for your birthday. Your grandma always gets you the worst gifts! Do you say:

   a. "Grandma! These are for kindergarteners! I've been skating for 4 years and I'll never use these."

   b. "Can I return these and use the money to get something that I *really* want?"

   c. "Thanks, Grandma. It was really nice of you to get me something."

7. This nasty kid at school just called you a freak. You know he's just a bully, but it still stinks to have him target you. Do you:

   a. wait until he walks by and stick out your foot so he lands flat on his face. SUCKER!

   b. get back at him by spreading a rumor that he's a bed-wetter.

   c. say, "Well, at least I don't go around ripping on people to feel good about myself!"

8. You really like to draw and hope that your rocket ship sketch will be picked for the school art show. Instead, another kid gets picked for a painting of his dog (*boring!*). Do you:

   a. tell the kid that if the teacher wasn't going blind, she'd have picked your drawing, since it was obviously better.

   b. say, "Nice painting, but I think your dog looks a little cross-eyed."

   c. congratulate him for getting picked, even though you're disappointed.

9. You're at your friend's house after school and you're invited to stay for dinner. You've had her mom's cooking before and it's AWFUL. Do you say:

a. "Just as long as we're not having that horrible meatloaf again!"

b. "Okay, but do you think we can order a pizza?"

c. "No thanks, my mom wants me home for dinner."

10. Your friend borrowed $10 from you two weeks ago and hasn't paid you back. Do you:

a. wait until he's not looking and fish through his backpack to see if you can just take the money from his wallet.

b. drop hints like "Don't you *hate* it when people borrow money and forget to pay you back?"

c. ask, "Hey, do you have the money I lent you to return to me yet?"

How'd You Do?

Give yourself **two points** for every **c** and **one point** for every **b**. Sorry, **no points** for every **a**! Add it all up and see how you did!

Watch out world, here I come! *(15–20 points)*
You have a pretty good sense of what to say and do already, which is good for your sake, and for those around you! Keep using your head and following your gut as you work your way through this book. You'll be in great shape to tackle the world and get what you want!

Ready...or not! *(8–14 points)*
You have an okay idea of how to handle yourself, but you don't always make the best decisions about what to say or do. Don't worry—that's where this book comes in! Read on to learn how to get through all kinds of sticky situations.

Help is on the way! *(0–7 points)*
Yikes! You have a knack for picking the *worst* possible thing to do when faced with everyday challenges. But with a little help, you can learn to do and say the right things more often. Keep on reading!

How to Get What You Want

You probably already have a good idea of how hard it can be to get what you want in life since you:

- are a kid
- don't make a lot of money, or the rules
- have to deal with a bunch of people who want (or don't want!) the same things as you, or who like to tell you what to do (like your teachers and parents).

Sounds familiar? Well, you can't change being a kid for the next few years (in fact, you probably have a ways to go!), and it's unlikely that you'll be president any time soon. So until then, **the trick is to know how to deal with the people you live with, including your folks, siblings, friends, even teachers**, and to make sure that you get what you want from them!

Ready to find out how? Read on!

HOW TO GET WHAT YOU WANT FROM YOUR FOLKS

"What I want I always get. I never have to wait for Christmas. I just scream and have a fit, and then my Daddy is so generous."
—A Spoiled Brat

If you're one of those kids who can *whine* your way into getting whatever you want from your folks, then you might not need this book (although you *might* need some more friends!). But, if you're like *most* people, you could probably use a few tips to turn "no" and "are you kidding me?" into "we'll see" or maybe even "sure, why not!" Whether you're asking for money, a pricey gadget, or to stay up—or out—later, here are some **tips for talking to your folks that will help you get what you want.**

The difference between getting what you want or getting a big "no way" from your folks can often be as simple as *when* you decide to talk to them. So, before hitting them up for anything, make sure you:

Have a clean record. If your room looks like the last friend to come visit was Hurricane Hugo, or if your dog did his thing on the carpet because you forgot to walk him, it's a good idea to *clean* up your act before asking your mom or dad for anything!

Check the stress. It's *not* a good time to talk about something you want if your dad's freaking out about car repairs, your mom's pulling out her hair over your aunt's wedding plans, or if they're *both* stressed out about anything related to *you*! Instead, approach them when they're not dealing with a disaster.

Choose your moment. If you start asking for things at a moment when your folks are busy, they might just say no because they don't have time to even *think* about it. If they look distracted, ask them when would be a good time to talk, rather than blurting out what you want right then and there. Or better yet, come back another time.

HOW TO ASK FOR MONEY

Of course, you know that money doesn't grow on trees, but wouldn't it be easier if it did? Then you wouldn't have to hit your folks up for some dough all the time, right? But, don't worry, there are things you *can* do to increase your chances of getting the cash you need to get the stuff you want.

Spend wisely.

Sure, you might want a new video game or a gigantic gum ball machine, but your folks might think they're a big waste of money. So, whenever you can, **ask them for money to pay for the things they're likely to want you to have,** like a new bike helmet or a book (and then use your stash of birthday cash or tooth fairy loot for the rest!).

Make a deal.

Offer to do something above and beyond your usual responsibilities in return for the money. Take on extra chores, help your younger brother with his homework, or give your mom a hand in the yard.

Show them the money.

Prove to your folks that you're responsible with their money. Keep track of your purchases and show them where you're spending the cash—they just might be impressed enough to give you more!

HOW TO GET SOMETHING EXPENSIVE

Are there better ways to let your folks know you want a new bike other than taping a photo of it to the fridge and hoping they take the hint, or bribing your little sister to say how much you deserve it for being such a great role model? Here are some ideas:

- **Don't act like your folks owe you something,** or that you somehow have a *right* to a new bike. That'll probably get you nothing but a "when I was your age, I had to walk seven miles to school" story—and who wants to listen (again) to that?

- **Don't act like you don't remember all the other things your folks have given you.** If you just got a new wardrobe (even if it *was* for *school*!), don't say that you haven't gotten *anything* new in "sooooo long." You'll lose points for acting ungrateful and that won't help your case!

- **Don't be overly dramatic** or act like it's a matter of life and death whether you get a new bike or not. Truth is, you *can* survive without one (as much as you'd like *not* to)—and your parents know it! Instead, explain how having a new bike will help you get to school on time, or how the bike you want has lots of good safety features.

- **Do offer to pay for half** of the bike with future earnings from your allowance, or with other money you'll save up, if you think it'll help.

When you're asking for something big

Don't Say: "I really need a new bike. All the other kids have nicer bikes than me!"

Do Say: "I could really use a bigger bike. My knees hit the handle bars on my old one, plus it's rusty and dented."

Don't Say: "It's only $200! You spent more than that fixing up your car!"

Do Say: "I know it's a lot of money, but I found a place where it's on sale this week for $200 instead of $250."

Don't Say: "I can't wait until my next birthday! That's months away!"

Do Say: "How about if I get this as my birthday present early? I promise I'll remember when my birthday comes around!"

Don't Say: "Fine! If you won't get it for me, I'll get it myself!"

Do Say: "If you can't afford it right now, can I try to earn the extra money by cleaning out the garage or pet-sitting?"

HOW TO ASK FOR MORE INDEPENDENCE

Sometimes what you want isn't anything money can buy, but a little more freedom—and being allowed to do new things—like going to bed later than your kid brother, sleeping over at a friend's house, or being dropped off at the mall with a friend and without a chaperone. **How do you get your folks to realize that you're not a little kid anymore and to let you do the stuff you want?**

- Imagine if your friend asked you for five favors all at once— you'd probably say no, right? **Try asking for only one new thing at a time—you'll increase the chances that your folks will agree to it.**

- Let your folks know that you know how to play it safe. Decide on rules for you to follow together, like calling to check in when you're out, or always telling them where you'll be and who you'll be with.

- Try out a new rule for a few weeks before making it permanent. Show your folks that you really *can* stay up an hour later at night and *still* get yourself up and ready for school on time the next day (it'll help your case if you can stay awake during math class, too!).

- **If your folks say "no way, Jose", don't cry or throw a tantrum (remember, the idea is for you to convince them that you're not a little kid anymore!).** Instead, calmly ask when they might be open to talking about the issue again, and then wait for the right time to bring it up. You just might blow them away by how mature you've become!

Top 10 things you should NOT say to your folks

Sure, you'll be tempted to blurt out one or more of these from time to time, but saying *any* of them will hurt your chances at *ever* getting what you want—so **zip the lips**!

1. "But you promised!"

2. "It's not fair!"

3. "But everyone else has it!"

4. "I never get anything I want!"

5. "You don't care about me!"

6. "I wish you weren't my mom/dad!"

7. "But why not?"

8. "This stinks!"

9. "If I don't get it, then…"

10. "But I *need* it!"

HOW TO GET WHAT YOU WANT FROM YOUR SIBLINGS

Brothers and sisters can come in handy at times (who else really understands how dumb your dad's jokes can be?), but they can also be a big pain—especially when you *both* want the *same things* at the *same time* and are always in each other's face! **As impossible as it may seem, there are ways to get what you want from them—whether it's the TV remote, or for them to go away—at least some of the time!**

HOW TO GET YOUR SHARE
OF THE REMOTE AND OTHER STUFF

You rush home to watch your favorite TV show—only to find your older sister snuggled up with the remote in the best seat in the house, watching soaps. You're psyched to check your e-mail and there she is on the computer, chatting on-line forever with her best friend. You've *really* got to go to the bathroom in the morning and...arghh!

She's in there drying her hair for half an hour! How do you get what you want from someone who *always* seems to get to it—and hog it—first?

Swap it.

For a quick fix, trade your sister half an hour playing with your hamster or a treasured possession while you watch your favorite TV show or surf the Internet.

Agree on it.

At a time when you guys are getting along, sit down and work out a "peace treaty" so that everyone can live together without battling. That is, **work out a schedule so that you both get equal time with shared stuff, like bathrooms, computers, and comfy chairs**. Base the schedule on different hours, days, weeks, or months, depending on what you're sharing.

Record it.

Once you come up with your peace treaty, put it in writing to make it official. Keep a record or chart of who gets to do what, so you'll remember what you agreed to.

RULE #1 IS WHOEVER GOES OVER THEIR HALF HOUR ON THE COMPUTER HAS TO GO TO SCHOOL WITH GREEN HAIR FOR THE DAY

Stick to it.

Make sure you guys figure out how to handle what happens when someone breaks a rule (like whoever goes over their bathroom time has to do the other person's chores!) and include that in your peace treaty. Then make sure to stick to your end of the bargain—unless you're willing to pay the penalty!

Tips for winning a battle with a sib

- **Never say "never".** Okay, he drives you crazy when he takes too long on the computer. But don't say that you *never* get to use it in an argument, since that's not likely to be true. Stick to the facts when you make your case, and be reasonable—it'll be harder for him to argue against you that way.

- **Fight fair.** Sure, you can threaten to hold her diary hostage, but odds are she'll come up with an equally nasty way to get back at you. **Don't stoop to dirty tricks, and keep the fight about the issue at hand.**

- **Don't tattle.** Telling on your brother isn't going to make him like you any more, or even get you any closer to what you want! Only bring an adult into the issue if you've tried every other option first. Who's to say you'll like what the grown-up says, anyway? Maybe she'll take your brother's side!

- **Don't get physical.** Sure, it's tempting to throw something when your sib acts like an obnoxious know-it-all, but that's the *worst* thing you can do. You'll *both* be angrier and probably *both* get in trouble, too, if the fists start flying.

HOW TO GET A LITTLE RESPECT, PEACE AND QUIET, AND PRIVACY

No matter how hard you try, you won't be able to stop your little bro or sis from wanting everything you have, wanting to do everything you do, and copying you all the time. But, you *can* do things to get them to stop taking your stuff, pestering you when your friends come over, and going through your room when you're not home. Take the quiz on the next page to see how good you are at getting what you want from your sibs!

1. Your kid brother always wants to borrow your hat because he thinks it's really cool. Do you:

    a. tell him no way, he has cooties, and you don't want to get them.

    b. tell him he has plenty of his own hats and that he doesn't need yours.

    c. tell your mom that he's bugging you and to get him to leave you alone.

    d. tell him he can wear it as long as he stops picking his nose around you.

2. Your little sis likes to go through your things when you're not home. You know she does this because you find her sticky little fingerprints on everything. Do you:

    a. go into her room and mess up her things.

    b. give her a lecture on the value of privacy.

    c. set up booby traps to dump water on her head when she opens the door.

    d. pretend to leave, wait until she goes into your room, and then nab her (it doesn't hurt if you scare the living daylights out of her, right?).

3. Your younger bro keeps barging into your room while you and your friend are trying to do homework together. Do you:

    a. yell at him to leave you alone.

    b. call him names until he cries.

    c. tell him you're playing hide and seek—and tell him to go hide.

    d. promise to play with him later if he leaves you alone now.

4. Your little sis always wants to do everything you do, which can be really annoying. Today, you're washing your dad's car for him. Do you:

    a. wait until she's occupied before going outside.

    b. spray her with the hose when she comes near you.

    c. tell your dad you can't work with her bugging you.

    d. teach her how to scrub the windows, then go and take a break.

If you answered **d** to all of the questions, you're a natural! When dealing with younger sibs, the trick is to outsmart them or to bargain to get what you want from them. Sometimes the stuff they want (like wanting to wear your hat) is no big deal to you, but can get you a lot in return! Why not let your little sis sit on your bed, if she agrees to *make* it first? Also, remember that most of the time, younger sibs bug you when they want your attention. So instead of trying to get them to go away (which can be a lot like trying to swat away a pesky fly), you might agree to spend some time with them in exchange for some peace and quiet when you want it. That way you'll get what you want (and everyone will be happier)!

HOW TO GET WHAT YOU WANT FROM YOUR FRIENDS

It's easy to have fun when you and your friends always agree on what to do, or when you enjoy the same things. But every now and then, even the friend you can count on to get the joke before you finish it, be the only one who will split a pineapple-and-hot-pepper pizza with you (*eww!*), and happily do whatever you're in the mood for, will want something different than you. So then what? Do you find yourself in a fight, find a new friend, or find a way to get what you want? You decide!

HOW TO CONVINCE A FRIEND TO DO WHAT YOU WANT

You've been counting down the days for the new movie about talking dogs to hit the theatre—but now your best bud tells you he's in the mood to go skateboarding instead. How do you get your friend to go to the flick with you?

1. Find out why your friend doesn't want to check out the film (or do whatever else it is you want to do). Maybe he's heard from other people that it was *doggone* awful. Or maybe he has an unexplainable fear of talking pooches.

2. Try to convince your friend to check out the movie with you. Tell him (if true) that when your cousin went to see it, he laughed so hard he cried. Say that everyone's going to be talking about it at school and this way he can join in on the laughs.

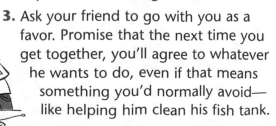

3. Ask your friend to go with you as a favor. Promise that the next time you get together, you'll agree to whatever he wants to do, even if that means something you'd normally avoid— like helping him clean his fish tank.

4. Think about what your friend wants to do, and how much fun it would be. Maybe you really would be just as happy to go skateboarding. If so, agree to go, in exchange for a trip to the movies next week (and try to get him to throw in the popcorn, too!).

5. Flip a coin. Whoever wins gets to choose what to do today, and the other gets to choose next time. You can't get more fair than that!

HOW TO GET WHAT YOU WANT FROM A BOSSY FRIEND

Do you have any friends who always want their own way, and somehow manage to get it? Do you find yourself wondering at times why you're even friends? Well, just because someone's bossy doesn't mean that she can't be a good friend—you just have to show her that you're not a pushover. Here are some tips on how to stand up for yourself and get what you want:

- **Be clear about what you want.** You can't blame someone for being bossy if you're *letting* it happen. Your friend can't guess what you want or read your mind, so say what you think!

- **Stick up for yourself.** Say that you're not going to hang out anymore, if you don't get to do what you want *some of* the time.

- **Follow through.** If you said you wouldn't play kickball with her if you didn't get to pick the teams this time, don't do it! After a while, even the bossiest person around will realize that you can't be pushed around.

> FIRST WE'LL EAT MY FAVORITE SNACK, PEANUT BUTTER AND SARDINES, THEN YOU'LL HELP ME WITH MY HOMEWORK AND THEN I'LL BEAT YOU AT CHECKERS

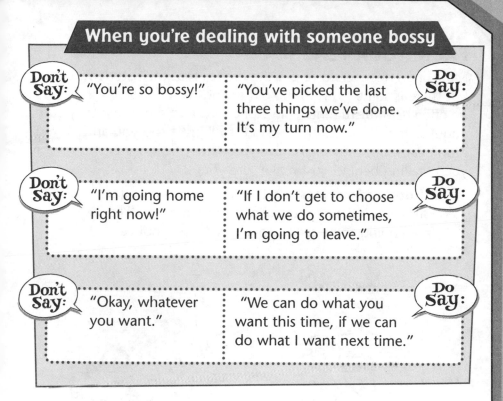

Don't Say: "You're so bossy!"

Do Say: "You've picked the last three things we've done. It's my turn now."

Don't Say: "I'm going home right now!"

Do Say: "If I don't get to choose what we do sometimes, I'm going to leave."

Don't Say: "Okay, whatever you want."

Do Say: "We can do what you want this time, if we can do what I want next time."

HOW TO GET WHAT YOU WANT FROM YOUR TEACHERS

So you're stuck with your teacher for the whole school year (and she's stuck with you!). You might think she's groovy (or you might think she's absolutely nuts). But no matter what you think of her, there are things that you probably want from your teacher, like getting good grades, and being one of the kids she likes (it never hurts to be a teacher's pet, right?). So, how do you do it? Pay attention to *this* lesson and find out!

I HOPE YOU LIKE APPLES MS. MCINTOSH

HOW TO GET GOOD GRADES FROM YOUR TEACHER

Most often, teachers give out the grades that their students earn. But there is some truth to the old saying "A for effort"—teachers *do* often reward students who work hard and show that they care about school. That doesn't mean they'll just hand you an "A" you didn't earn, but they *might* give you extra credit or help you out if you're falling behind. Just make sure you:

- **Show up for class.** That sounds like a no-brainer, right? But if you miss a lot of school for sketchy reasons (like pretending to be sick!), your teacher will notice.

- **Be on time.** That doesn't mean running in breathless just when the bell rings and mooching some paper and a pen off the kid next to you five minutes later. Get to class a few minutes early and be prepared to start working when the bell rings.

- **Do your homework.** And even if your dog really *did* eat your homework, do it again! Odds are, your teacher's already heard every excuse in the book!

- **Pay attention.** If you're snoozing or twiddling your thumbs during class, your teacher won't be as sympathetic when you don't understand something.

- **Ask for help.** If you really *were* concentrating and still don't understand a lesson (or a whole unit!), ask your teacher to help you "get it" before or after school, or during recess. That'll really show you care.

What to do when you don't know the answer

It's math class and you're totally *not* getting the word problems, which sound like a bunch of mumbo jumbo to you. Ms. Percent is going over last night's homework, and you've gotten all the answers wrong so far. You slide down into your chair, hoping that if she doesn't see you, she won't call on you. But sure enough, her eyes zero in on you and she calls out your name for the next answer. What do you do?!?

a. Slide down further under the desk so she thinks you've disappeared.

b. Tell her you need to go to the bathroom really, *reeeaaally* badly and run out of the room.

c. Stare at her blankly for several painfully slow seconds until she gives up on you and calls on someone else.

d. Tell her you don't know the answer.

What's the right answer? You got it: **d**! In this sitch, the best thing to do is to simply admit, "I don't know." If you want, you can mention that you didn't understand the lesson, but that you'll do your best to catch up and understand what the answer should be. The *worst* thing you can do is to just sit there in silence as she stares at you and as she— and everyone else in class—waits to hear what you'll say!

NEXT QUESTION, COREY?

HOW TO GET YOUR TEACHER TO LIKE YOU

Think getting your teacher to like you is all about bringing a shiny red apple to school on the first day? Or being the one who rats out the kid who threw the spitball? Or being a show-off student? Nope! Teachers usually don't fall for the kids who bribe or tattle or sneer their way to the top. Instead, teacher's pets are usually the kids who:

- **Like to learn.** Think about it— teachers spend their lives trying to get kids to learn stuff (whether they do or not!). Obviously, they'll like the kids who make their efforts seem worth it. Wouldn't you?

- **Give a teacher respect.** Teachers really *do* have eyes behind their heads, and they always manage to find out about the kids who say nasty stuff about them, right? Be one of the ones who treats them well to their faces *and* behind their backs.

- **Follow the rules.** It's a pain to have to tell a kid over and over again not to talk, chew gum, or sleep in class. Remember, even if you almost find yourself calling her "mom" once in a while, your teacher is *not* a parent who'll love you no matter how many times you try her patience (maybe her own kids can expect that, but not you!).

- **Participate in class.** Why's it so important to answer your teacher's questions? She knows the answers already anyway, right? It shows that you're enthusiastic about what you're learning (which makes her job easier, and it makes her feel good that she's doing a good job teaching).

How to Mean What You Say

You spend a lot of time talking to people, but how often do you say something that really counts? Sometimes it's not enough to have a bunch of sounds coming out of your mouth—you need the words you use to *work for you* so that you get the things you want. **Here you'll get the scoop on what to say to make sure other people take you seriously—whether you want to get your money's worth, to speak the truth even if it hurts, to say "no" like you mean it, or to get someone to forgive you.** Make sure that you're not just making noise, but that you're being *heard*!

WHAT TO SAY TO GROWN-UPS WHO TREAT YOU LIKE A KID

Ever get the feeling that some of the grown-ups in your life don't take you seriously, or, that they try to take advantage of you just because you're a kid? Bet you can't wait to be older and get the respect you deserve, right? Well, you don't need to wait *that* long! You can demand the same courtesy as the next person, no matter how much bigger or older they are than you. What would you do in the following sitch?

You've been patiently standing in a super-long line at a store during a one-day sale that has attracted crazy holiday shoppers from all over the place. While you're waiting, a woman cuts directly in front of you. Do you say:

a. Nothing. This lady's old enough to be your grandmother and you should just let her in ahead of you, right?

b. "Hey everyone, she's cutting!"

c. "Look lady, are you *blind*? There's a line!"

d. "Excuse me, maybe you didn't see me, but I've been waiting here."

If you answered **d**, you're on the right track. Be polite but direct, and stand up for yourself! That way, there's a good chance that the person will apologize and go to the end of the line where she belongs. And if she doesn't for some reason, bring it up to the salesperson. Sometimes, folks are just plain rude, and you get points for sticking up for yourself, whether you get what you want or not!

EXCUSE ME, MAYBE YOU DIDN'T SEE ME IN LINE, BUT I WAS HERE FIRST

Tips for speaking to adults so that they take you seriously

Whether it's your dad, mom, doctor, bus driver, shoe salesperson, or anyone else, it'll help you to be understood and taken seriously by adults if you:

- Try to sound more like *they* do than like a kid your own age.

- Watch your tone of voice. If you're whining or sound like a baby, most adults will treat you like one!

- Use terms of respect like "sir" or "ma'am" and always refer to adults by their correct title, whether it's "officer," "doctor," or just "Mr." or "Ms." Even if you *think* it sounds old fashioned, it shows adults you're aware of their status, and they'll be more likely to treat you politely in return. Of course, if they say, "Oh, please call me Lindsay, instead of Ms. Biggal," then by all means, go ahead!

WHAT TO SAY WHEN YOU'VE BOUGHT A PIECE OF JUNK

Your new rollerblade lost a wheel, your brand-new puzzle is missing a piece out of the box, your video game controller won't move to the left—it's a bummer when something you buy either doesn't work right, or breaks right after you get it. But don't toss it yet! First, try to get it fixed or get your money back by speaking up and taking these steps to getting what should be coming to you:

1. **Call or visit the place** where you purchased the stuff and explain the problem. You'll find out right away if the store is willing to return or replace the product for you (be sure to take your receipt along!).

2. If the store where you purchased the product can't help you out, **contact the business** that makes it (also known as the manufacturer). There should be a 1–800 number, customer service line, or e-mail address that you can use to ask for assistance (find this on the item itself, or on its packaging, or ask the place where you bought it).

WHEN THE ROBOT KEPT SAYING "UH OH" INSTEAD OF "MY NAME IS ROB THE ROBOT", I KNEW SOMETHING WAS WRONG WITH IT!

3. **Find out if the product is under warranty** or has a satisfaction guarantee, which means that you can send it back to be replaced or fixed.

4. **Take note of the name of the person you spoke to,** plus the date and time, so that you can refer to the conversation later if you need to.

5. If nothing is done, or if you're told that you can't be helped, **write a letter** of complaint to the company headquarters—even to the company's president—or contact a consumer affairs office. In the letter, clearly explain what you've done so far, including details of where and when you bought the item, the people you've spoken to since then, and why you're not satisfied. Type this up if you can, and keep a copy of it.

6. **Wait and see** what happens. You might get a response, or you might not. At the very least, the company has a record of your complaint, and you've made yourself heard—which counts for something!

WHAT TO SAY WHEN YOU GET A HAIRCUT YOU HATE

You asked the hairdresser to give your hair a slight trim, only to step off the chair looking like you tried cutting your own hair—blindfolded! It's a lot shorter than you asked for, and it's not even cut evenly! You want to scream, or cry, or stick your head in the sand, but instead you get up, pay the fee, add a tip, and leave, right? Wrong! Just like when you've bought a product, you're entitled to let someone know if you don't think you got your money's worth for a service you've received, so:

OH NO, I DIDN'T ASK TO LOOK LIKE HER!

- Before paying a cent, **politely explain why the haircut you got isn't what you asked for** and why it isn't what you want.

- **Ask the stylist** to try to do whatever possible **to fix your hair** to make it look better.

- If you get nowhere with the stylist, **ask to speak to a manager** and see if she can get you **another stylist** to fix your hair, give you a **discount** on the haircut you already got (or say it's at no charge), provide you with a coupon for a **free haircut** next time, or at least lend you a wig (ha, ha)!

- Remember to **be respectful, but assertive**. Most of the time, someone working in a service-oriented job will try to make things better for you, because there's *nothing* worse for a business than an unhappy customer who likes to spread the word around!

SURVIVAL TIP!

When you're at a restaurant and don't get what you ordered (or find that the stuff sitting on your plate is cold when it's supposed to be hot, or inedible), speak up! Don't let a snobby or rude waiter intimidate you into eating what you don't want. *Warning: Do not try this at home!*

HOW TO ASK FOR SOMETHING THAT BELONGS TO YOU

It's been ages since you lent your friend a prized possession and now you want it back. You've already let him hold on to it for much longer than you had in mind, and you're beginning to wonder if he thinks it was a gift (it wasn't!). So how do you ask for something back that belongs to you without seeming rude?

- **Be direct.** Simply say, "Hey, if you're done with my video game, I'd like to have it back now, please."

- **Don't feel like you need to apologize.** It always helps to be friendly, but there's no need to say sorry for wanting your stuff back. (If anything, your friend should be the one to apologize for not returning it before you had to ask!)

- **Make it easy.** If your friend keeps forgetting to bring you what you want back, offer to stop by his place and pick it up.

- **Offer a trade**. If you have something of his, say "Thanks for lending me your baseball cards. Do you have my board game? We can trade back now."

- If you've already tried asking once or twice, with no luck, **ask again in a different way, or by saying something different**. This time, say that you promised to lend it to someone *else* who's waiting for it, or mention that it was a gift from your mom and she's wondering where it went.

TO: Peter
From: Paul
You've got my stuff!

HOW TO ASK SOMEONE FOR MONEY THAT THEY OWE YOU

If someone said you'd get $1 million for being the first person to get to the bank and demand it (no, it's not a stickup—the money's free for whoever asks!), you'd have no problem racing over there and asking a total stranger for the money, right? Then why is it so much harder to ask your bud for the five bucks he owes you? For some reason, a lot of people feel awkward in this type of sitch because they don't want to seem greedy or ungenerous. What would you do in the following scenario?

You've just dog-sat three of the friskiest pups you've ever known for four exhausting days, including jogs in the park and marathon Frisbee sessions. When their owner finally gets back to town, he thanks you and gives you a check for $21, as you hand over the leashes. But then you realize you should have gotten $28, since you had agreed to a rate of $7 a day. What do you do?

a. Take the money and be happy that you're $21 richer than you were before.

b. Wait until the next time you see the owner, and *then* ask for the extra money he owes you.

c. Stomp out of the house without taking anything.

d. Speak up right away, tell the owner that he made a mistake, and politely ask for the correct amount.

If you answered **d**, you've got the right idea! Don't settle for less than what you've earned for your hard work. If you wait to speak up, you run the risk that your customer won't remember exactly how much he gave you later, or what he originally agreed to pay. And though it can be tough to do, it can be more convincing to get what you agreed to if you speak up right then and there. So, say something **now**—in a polite and business-like way—and get what you've earned!

If you find yourself in this situation...	Say this...
Your friend borrowed five dollars from you at the movies two months ago.	"Hey, do you have the five bucks I lent you two months back? I could really use it now!"
You raked your neighbor's lawn and she didn't have the cash to pay you last week.	"Hi Mrs. Green, is it a good time for me to collect my leaf-raking fee from you?"
Your sister asks to borrow ten dollars from you, but she *still* hasn't paid you the money she borrowed from you last time.	"I was hoping you'd pay me back the money you borrowed at the mall before I lend you any more. When can you pay me back?"

How to Say "No" Like You Mean It!

You've been hearing the word "no" for as long as you can remember—like "that's a no-no" when you tried to stick your finger in the electrical outlet as a baby, "nooooo!" when you gave your teddy bear a bath in the toilet as a tot, "no way, buddy!" when you asked if you could stay up late to watch TV on a school night just last week. So why is it, after all your experience with the word "no," that it's still so hard sometimes to say it to *other* people?

It could be that sometimes you're afraid that people will feel rejected, think you don't like them, or get angry if you don't give them what they want. Or you might think that being a nice person means putting other people's needs above your own. That's certainly true *some* of the time. But at other times, by agreeing to do things you don't want, you're not being fair to yourself! And you might even end up resenting the people you're being nice to in the long run, which means no one wins! Here are some tips for saying "no" as well as the pros do—your folks, that is!

When...	Try saying no like this...
That weird kid from science class invites you over to watch him feed his pet insects and paint rocks, but you really don't want to spend any more time with him than you already do at school.	Simply say "no, thank you," if you're not interested. If you want, you can add a reason why you're busy (but don't give a lame excuse like "I've got to wash my hair!").
Your friend wants you to help her with her social studies project, but you still have a lot of your own homework left.	Say that you'd like to help, but that you have your own work to do. Suggest other ways for her to get the help she needs. "I'm sorry, but I'm behind on my own work. Why don't you ask Ben if he can help?"
Your sister wants you to walk the dog for her and reminds you that you owe her a favor from last week. You want to help her out, but you're getting late for school.	Offer to help out later to repay your favor, and point out that she should have given you a heads up so that you could have gotten ready earlier. "I can walk him for you when I get back from school, if you want. I would've done it this morning, if you had told me sooner."

When...	Try saying no like this...
Your friend has asked you to get together three times in the past two weeks, and each time you've been busy. Now he's asking you to go out a fourth time.	It's okay to say no again, but offer another time to get together so he doesn't think you're deliberately avoiding him. Say something like, "I can't believe it, but I'm busy again! How about we hang out next Saturday at my place?"
Your neighbor asks you to smoke with him, but you don't want to.	Look the person straight in the eye, and say "no." Follow it up by saying what could happen (like, "we could get caught"). Add another reason like "my dad would kill me if he found out" or "I've got asthma," if you need to.

WHAT TO SAY WHEN SOMEONE WON'T TAKE NO FOR AN ANSWER

You've already said "no" to your friend and given him all the reasons why you don't do things like smoke, skip school, or forge your parent's signature. But he's still pushing you and pressuring you by saying you're not a *real* friend, and calling you a loser. You know you've always been a good friend, and last time you checked you were actually pretty cool, but it still makes you feel bad to hear your friend say mean things about you. So what should you do?

- Realize that your friend is the one acting like a loser by trying to push you to do something you don't want to do.
- Say "no" again, and if he still doesn't get it, say it again in as many different ways as you can, like, "I don't want to," "I think that's a bad idea," or "no way."
- Ask, "Why should I?" and make *him* try to come up with a good reason for you to do it. If he does, tell him that the reason isn't good enough for you!
- Come up with a better idea of something to do. Say, "I'm going to the park to shoot some hoops. If you want to join me, come on over, because that's where I'll be."
- Walk away to a place where you're comfortable, like maybe around another group of kids who are doing something you like.
- Turn to an adult you can trust if things get nasty, or if you feel yourself starting to give in to the pressure.

If English doesn't work, try saying "no" in another language!

NO, NON, NEIN, NYIT, LA, NAHEEN, LO, MHAI, IiE

Spanish: No

French: Non (pronounced "no")

German: Nein (pronounced "nine")

Russian: Nyit (pronounced "neeyit")

Hebrew: Lo

Arabic: La (pronounced "la" as in ladder)

Urdu: Naheen (pronounced "nay-hee")

Chinese: Mhai (pronounced "my")

Japanese: Iie (pronounced "ee-eh")

How NOT to Say What You Mean!

When you were a little kid and didn't know how to express yourself well, you cried, screamed, and maybe even hit, kicked, or bit people to get what you wanted, or to let others know how you felt. Hopefully, as you grew older, you learned to use words to get your point across, instead of tears or teeth! That doesn't mean you still don't get angry from time to time—there's nothing wrong with that, as long as you **let someone know why you're angry in a mature way (that way, you don't need to feel bad or apologize for your anger later)**. But there *is*

WAHHHH!!

something wrong with losing your self-control and handling things the same way you did as a toddler, and doing things like yelling, saying nasty things, or hitting or shoving someone. What can you do when you're so angry you think you're going to blow your top?

Time Out!

- Punch some pillows as hard as you can.
- Go outside and kick a ball around or whack some baseballs.
- Count backwards from 100 to 1.

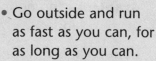

59, 58, 57...

- Go outside and run as fast as you can, for as long as you can.
- Hug a pet (a person will do fine, too!).
- Cry it out in private.
- Tell someone who isn't connected to the problem how you feel about it.

OOPS! What To Say *After* You've Put Your Foot In Your Mouth

Everyone gets a good taste of their foot in their mouth occasionally. So, how in the world do you recover when you've said something so stupid you wish the ground would just open up and swallow you whole? The best way to handle it is to realize what you've done, apologize if necessary, and use a bit of humor whenever possible. **People will be more likely to forgive you if they see that you're truly embarrassed or surprised by what you said**, rather than playing it cool, pretending nothing happened, or acting like you don't care.

When you...	Try saying...
Ask your friend if you can come over and walk her dog, forgetting that her pooch pal Rufus was put to sleep last week.	"I'm sorry, I didn't mean to be insensitive. Somehow, I completely forgot."
Ask your friend why he didn't come to the party Saturday night, and he tells you he wasn't invited.	"I'm sorry, I just thought you'd be there since everyone likes to have you at a party."
Complain about how horrible the new substitute teacher is to the girl next to you in the lunch line, only to find out that the sub is her mother!	"I can't believe I said that. I'm sure your mom's cool. I was just bent out of shape because she told me to stop talking in class and it wasn't me talking."

OUCH! WHAT TO SAY WHEN THE TRUTH HURTS

Everyone has moments when they'd rather say something else, because they know the truth isn't exactly what someone else wants to hear. **Some people speak their minds no matter what the cost, while others bend the truth a little here and there to spare someone's feelings** and use what are called "white lies". Where do you fit in? Try this quiz and see for yourself!

POP QUIZ SAY IT OR SAVE IT?

1. Your sister comes back from getting a haircut, which looks like a gigantic mushroom sprouted on top of her head. She spins around for you to see every angle of her new 'do and asks how she looks.

Do you:

a. tell her *exactly* what you think, mushroom and all.

b. tell her she looks great, and that everyone's going to want to get the same look.

c. tell her that she looks nice.

HOW DO I LOOK?

2. Your friend was grounded last weekend and wasn't allowed to go to the movies with you and your buds. The rest of you had a blast—it was the best movie you saw all year. When your friend asks how it was later, do you say:

    a. "It was the best! You would've loved it."

    b. "We didn't end up going."

    c. "It was okay."

3. You're at the fabric store with your mom, wondering if this is the worst form of torture known to humans. She shows you the *millionth* choice of cloth for the new curtains she's making. "Isn't this lovely?" she asks. It looks the same as the last twenty ones you've seen, and you couldn't care less. Do you say:

    a. "Mom, this is so *boring*! Can we go home now?"

b. "It's perfect! I love it."

    c. "If you like it, I think it'll work."

4. Your Dad's vegetarian cousin is visiting from out of town. He whips up an omelet made with tofu and sprouts that smells like old sneakers, and he insists you take a bite. It tastes as bad as it smells. Do you:

    a. run over to the sink and spit it out.

    b. ask for seconds.

    c. say "mmm" and drink some juice as quickly as you can.

5. Your best friend is going to try out for the soccer team. You've seen him play and know that he doesn't have a chance in the world, considering his skills (tennis is really his game) and the level of competition.

Do you:

a. tell him that he'll never make the soccer team.

b. wish him good luck.

c. tell him that he could be captain of the tennis team, if he tried out for that instead.

If most of your answers are **a**, you're a believer in telling the truth, the whole truth, and nothing but the truth! You prefer to tell it like it is—no matter how that makes others feel. Even though it's true that honesty is usually the best policy, sometimes a white lie here and there can actually be the nicer thing to do. It's all about using your judgment to decide what to do in each situation. If you're convinced that—like George Washington—you "cannot tell a lie" no matter what, then make sure that you do it gently because sometimes it's not what you say, but *how* you say it that counts!

If most of your answers are **b**, you don't have a problem telling little white lies, and maybe *bigger* ones, too! Sometimes it's easy to go overboard, beyond just being polite, to where you're handing out bad advice. Remember that, although it's nice to think of other people's feelings, it's also important to not always tell them only what they want to hear—for their sake. In the long run, people appreciate honesty—and turn to others who give them their real opinions.

If most of your answers are **c**, you know it's important to tell the truth, but also to be considerate of other people's feelings. You might tell a white lie or choose not to say anything at times so that someone doesn't get hurt. You've got a good idea of how to handle most sticky situations, so continue to use common sense on how and when to make your real feelings known.

WHEN TO USE THE LITTLE WHITE LIE

White lies are harmless most of
the time, and in some cases, they
might even be your best bet,
especially when:

You're being polite. Why tell
your little brother that his drawing
of a spaceship looks like a worm?
Go ahead and say it's awesome!

It's a matter of taste. Your friend
may *think* that her brownies are the best at the bake sale, even if
you think they taste like sawdust! Why not let her feel good about
her dessert—as long as she's the one who eats all the leftovers!

Someone feels bad. Your friend tripped across the stage during
the school's choir performance. He's embarrassed enough, so it's
okay to say that hardly anyone noticed, even if everyone *was*
talking about it. Why make him feel worse than he already does?

WHEN TO TELL THE TRUTH

Okay, so now that you've mastered the white lie, what about when
nothing but the whole truth will do? That's where it gets tricky!
Even though it might be harder than fibbing, sometimes the better
choice is to be upfront and honest. When? Basically, whenever what

you have to say will make a
difference or means something.
Make sure to *always* be truthful
in these situations:

- **If people you care about do
  things that make them look
  stupid, tell them.** It doesn't
  matter if they're wearing their
  shirt buttoned wrong, or
  walking around with a piece
  of spinach stuck in their teeth.
  You'd want them to stop
  you from doing something
  humiliating, right? So do
  the same for them!

43

- **When white lies start growing into bigger lies.**
You can keep telling your musically challenged cousin you
think he has real talent and should join a band, but what
about when he decides to perform at the school's talent
night and you *know* he'll get booed off the stage? Stop
him now, before the rotten tomatoes start flying!

- **When you have an opinion on something that
counts.** White lies work fine when you don't care about
something one way or the other, or when it's not something
important, but when you *do* feel strongly about something,
you owe it to yourself to speak your mind.

HOW TO SPEAK THE TRUTH TO SOMEONE WHO WON'T WANT TO HEAR IT

You've got to tell your friend that she's making a fool of herself
at her new school by pretending to have a German accent, even
though she grew up in Pittsburgh. Or you have to break it to your
friend that, because he swears at your house, your folks think he's
a rude kid with a gutter mouth and they won't let you hang out
with him anymore. It's never easy to tell people stuff you know
they won't want to hear, so what do you do?

1. Tell the person you have something to say, even
though (and tell them this) it's hard for you to say it.

2. Take a deep breath.

3. Look the person in the eye.

4. Say that you think being honest
is important in this sitch.

5. Come out with whatever you
have to say as directly as you
can (you can be kind, but don't
beat around the bush—that just
makes things drag on!).

6. Move away quickly after you say it,
in case they decide to charge
at you. (*Just kidding!* Most people
will appreciate your honesty, as
long as you aren't being nasty or making fun of them!)

THIS IS HARD FOR ME TO SAY, BUT....

?

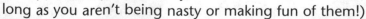

HOW TO STRETCH THE TRUTH WHEN YOU HATE A GIFT

You grab the gift Aunt Jean hands you with excitement. It feels just heavy enough to be the mini-camcorder you've been eyeing (and dropping hints about). You tear open the present, and find—what? A pair of brass monkey bookends? You've got to be kidding! Aunt Jean is smiling at you, waiting for your reaction. What do you say? Do you say what you *really* think, or tell a white lie?

When it comes to a gift, there's only one thing you can do: hide your unhappy surprise, disgust, or disappointment, and simply say "thank you" as warmly and sincerely as you can. If you can manage it, add another line like "that's really nice of you" or "this is too much" (no one needs to know that in your head you're thinking, "oh yeah, *waaaay* too much!").

Wondering why it's not a good idea to say thanks and look as disappointed as you feel? Because, even if it stinks, Aunt Jean might have put a lot of thought into that gift, thinking that you'd love it. By thanking her graciously, you'll make her feel good about her effort, and—just as importantly, perhaps—not blow your chances of getting another gift from her in the future! Who knows, maybe *next* time, she'll actually get you something you really want!

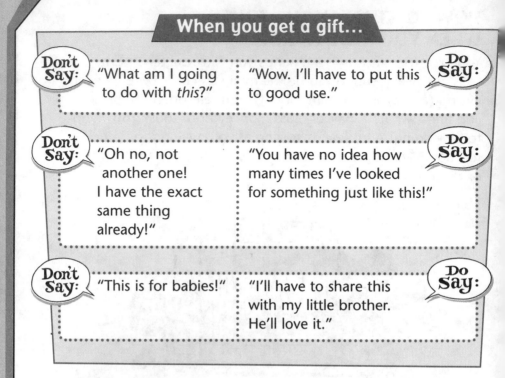

When you get a gift...

Don't Say: "What am I going to do with *this*?"

Do Say: "Wow. I'll have to put this to good use."

Don't Say: "Oh no, not another one! I have the exact same thing already!"

Do Say: "You have no idea how many times I've looked for something just like this!"

Don't Say: "This is for babies!"

Do Say: "I'll have to share this with my little brother. He'll love it."

HOW TO WRITE A THANK-YOU NOTE (WITHOUT BEING UNTRUTHFUL) FOR A GIFT YOU DON'T LIKE

It's hard enough finding a few polite words to say when you're face to face with someone who got you the worst gift ever! What do you do when you have to write an *entire* thank-you note about something you don't like, don't want, and don't know what to say about?

- **Mention the gift by name.** Instead of saying "thanks for the gift," say, "thanks for the brass monkey bookends."

- **Say how you'll use it**, or at least mention that they'll come in handy (and leave out the part about using them to prop up your bike in the garage!).

- **Don't overdo it.** Avoid going on and on about how you love the gift, if you don't. Apart from sounding fake, you might just encourage someone to get you a pair of brass *elephant* bookends next year!

Dear Grandma,
Thanks for sending me the thermal underwear for my Birthday. I'll be sure to wear them when it gets colder. It was nice of you to think of how to keep me warm! I hope to see you soon.
Love,
Zach

• **Focus on the person doing the giving.** Mention how nice it was to be thought of, and how thoughtful it was for the person to get you a gift. Here's an example:

Dear Uncle Moses,
Thanks for the fifth grade homework practice book. It'll sure come in handy when I get to fifth grade and feel like doing some extra work! Thanks for thinking of me!
Love, Matty.

Ten words you can use to describe a gift you don't like

"That's so...uh...*interesting*!" When you can't find the right word, sometimes "interesting" is all that comes to mind. Next time you find yourself fumbling for a polite adjective, try one of these:

1. Unique
2. Extraordinary
3. Special
4. Original
5. Remarkable
6. Fascinating
7. Unusual
8. Fantastic
9. Excellent
10. Exciting

WOW, THESE ARE REALLY... UNIQUE

HOW TO SAY SORRY LIKE YOU MEAN IT!

One of the hardest things to say to someone is "I'm sorry." That's probably why so many people are so bad at it! And a really pathetic apology can even be worse than not saying anything at all, so make sure you avoid these common mistakes:

When you say...	The other person hears...
"I think you're making a big deal about nothing."	"I'm not really sorry and, if anything, I think this is *your* fault!"
"I know I was late today, but you're always late whenever we meet up."	"You don't really deserve an apology for this, since you always do the *same thing* to me."
"I'm sorry, but I'm not sure how I hurt your feelings. You shouldn't be so sensitive."	"I don't really see how I hurt your feelings, but I'll just say sorry because you're being a big baby."
"Well, even if I did embarrass you, I was just kidding around."	"I didn't do anything to be sorry for because I was just trying to be funny, so whatever."
"I guess I shouldn't have taken your watch without asking, but you always hog the remote."	"You never apologize to me, so why should I say sorry to you?"

HOW TO GIVE AN APOLOGY THAT WORKS

The best way to make sure your apology is accepted is to make sure it *sounds* like you mean it!

1. Don't make excuses. There's a difference between giving someone a **real reason** for why you did or didn't do something and making up a **lame story**. People can usually tell the difference—and, if you're just making up excuses, it's just as bad as *not* apologizing at all!

2. **Don't try to stick the blame on someone else** for what you did by saying things like "He made me do it!" Everyone knows that no one can *make* you do anything (just ask your mom! She'll tell you she can't get you to clean your room!).

3. **Don't blame the other person for the way he feels.** If you did something to make someone feel bad, *you* are the one responsible to make it better.

4. **Avoid bringing up another issue** that has nothing to do with what you're saying sorry for (and avoid criticizing the person you're apologizing to, no matter how many *other* things he's done in the past to make you nuts). Stick to the issue at hand.

I SAID I'M SORRY!

5. Only say sorry when you actually know what you're apologizing for. It doesn't make a whole lot of sense to say *sorry* before you even understand why someone's upset. And, chances are good it'll make the person even angrier when he realizes that you can't *possibly* mean a word you're saying!

6. Be real. Even if you *say* all the right things, it won't count if you contradict yourself by shrugging, smirking, or having a nasty I-don't-mean-it tone of voice—as tempting as that might be!

7. Only apologize for things that really *are* your fault. If you're one of those people who *always* says sorry about *everything* (like when the weather spoils your hike, or because someone's favorite football team lost), your real apologies won't mean as much.

8. Don't make empty promises. Only say that you won't raid your sister's candy stash anymore if you *really* won't do it again! If you know your sweet tooth is going to get the best of you sooner or later, it's better to stick to "I'll *try* not to take your gum balls again!"

SURVIVAL TIP!

Make your apology count more by timing it right. If you've broken your dad's new watch, admit it *before* he finds it himself and comes yelling to find out what happened! You'll get points for being brave and confessing without getting caught first.

UM, DAD, REMEMBER THAT WATCH MOM GOT YOU FOR YOUR ANNIVERSARY?

What to do when saying sorry isn't enough

Sometimes even the perfect "sorry" isn't enough to fix everything. It's always a good place to start, but you may need to do more to make it up to someone (depending on how bad what you did was in the first place!).

- If you've lost or broken something that belongs to someone else, try to **fix it, replace it,** or offer to **pay for it.**

- If you did something you know was wrong—like lying or breaking a rule—**don't do it again!** Slowly, you'll begin to win back the trust you lost.

- If you didn't do something you were supposed to do, **get into gear and do it!**

- If you've hurt people's feelings, go out of your way to **do something nice for them.**

- **Give the person time** to forgive you and be patient. The worst thing you can do is to pester someone who's deciding whether or not to like you again!

Don't you just hate it when you're caught off guard and find that you're completely lost for words? Life is full of moments when you want to say something but aren't sure exactly how to get it out, like when you're meeting someone for the first time, don't remember a name, realize you caught someone in a lie, receive a compliment or an insult you weren't prepared for, and more! You can't stop life from throwing surprises at you, but **you can learn some tricks to help you get through the times when you're stammering, sputtering, or speechless!**

UHHH... UM

WHAT TO SAY WHEN YOU'RE MEETING SOMEONE NEW

HI, I'M JORDAN

It's easy! Just do this:

1. Smile.

2. Extend your hand (but only if you're in a formal setting—you don't see too many kids shaking hands with each other at school, right?).

3. Say, "I'm (say your name), what's yours?"

4. Strike up a conversation.

HOW TO MASTER THE ART OF SMALL TALK

You're stuck entertaining the shyest kid you've ever met during your mom's lunch party and don't know how you're going to survive the next two hours. You're at the pool and meet a nice kid you'd like to get to know better, but after saying hi, there's an awkward silence that makes you want to run and hide in the deep end. You're sitting next to a new kid at lunch and want to make him feel welcome, but you can't think of anything to say, as you're staring speechless at your peanut butter sandwich.

How do you start up a good conversation and keep it going?

- **Don't worry** about thinking of something clever or funny to say. Instead, keep it simple and start off by asking the person a question.

- **Choose a question** that requires more than a "yes" or "no" answer. If you say something like, "Are you new around here?" you might just get a "yup" as your reply. But if you say, "I heard you're new to the area, what brings you here?" you'll open up a conversation.

- **Use whatever info you get** about the person to ask him more questions, and to keep the conversation rolling. That's a lot easier than thinking of a bunch of different new topics to talk about.

- **Don't worry about appearing nosy** (and don't *be* nosy—keep the questions general and not too personal!). Most people *love* to talk about themselves, especially to somebody who seems interested in everything they have to say.

- **Don't go on and on about yourself too much**, but be open and share things if the other person asks. It helps if what you talk about ties into what you've already learned about the person.

- **Try to find something you both have in common**, but don't panic if you end up being completely different in every way imaginable. You can *still* have a great time talking— and maybe even become friends.

I LIKE COMIC BOOKS, PLAYING BASKETBALL AND BANANA SPLITS

OH REALLY, WELL I LIKE ENCYCLOPEDIAS, AND BASEBALL AND I'M ALLERGIC TO BANANAS!

- **Be yourself.** If you have something silly, funny, or smart to say—say it! Loosen up and have fun, and most people you're talking to will follow your lead.

SURVIVAL TIP!

It's a no-brainer: you'll have more to talk about if you do *more*! Get involved in activities and hobbies, read books, and learn about lots of different stuff. Soon enough, you'll find yourself full of fascinating, observant, or brilliant things to talk about!

10 Conversation Starters

1. What was your old neighborhood like?

2. What kind of music do you listen to?

3. Your sneakers are really cool, where did you get them?

4. Do you like our new bus driver?

5. Do you watch scary movies? Have you seen *Attack of the Potato People*?

6. Is this the worst school lunch you've ever had?

7. What do you think about the new after-school gym program?

8. Did you hear about the really smart kid in 7th grade who skipped two grades?

9. What was the last really good book you read?

10. Have you tried the new banana split cereal that's out?

You can always find something to talk about! What's the most talked-about topic ever? (Look outside for a hint.) You got it—the weather! Whether it's your mom reminding you to zip up, your coach wondering if the game's going to be cancelled, your dog whining about a thunderstorm, or you and your friends hoping for a snow day, you can *always* make small talk with just about anyone, anywhere, about the heat, rain, sleet, hail, wind, cold, sunshine, or snow!

HOW TO KNOW WHAT YOUR BODY LANGUAGE IS SAYING

Even if your lips are saying all the right things, the rest of your body might be contradicting them! Don't let your body language get the best of you, and be aware of what you're *really* saying to the people around you by keeping these tips in mind:

When you're...	What it says to the person you're talking to
Smiling at a new person	"Hi, I'm happy to meet/see you!"
Smiling and giggling the whole time you're talking to a new person	"I'm really nervous."
Standing or sitting with your arms open or at your side	"I'm a friendly and open person, and interested in getting to know you."
Standing or sitting with your arms crossed	"I'm a closed person and a bit defensive. Don't get too close!"
Leaning forward while someone is speaking	"I'm interested in what you have to say, and I don't want to miss a word."
Yawning a lot when someone is talking	"You're boring me. I'm ready to take a nap."
Standing close to someone while you're speaking	"I'm not afraid of you—and I'm confident that I smell good!"
Standing *too* close to someone	"I'm kinda creepy and I don't respect your personal space!"
Looking away or in another direction while someone speaks to you	"Yawn! Is there something else more interesting going on over there?"

Body language doesn't always translate!

Body language means different things around the world! The same gestures and signals you'd use to communicate with others in your home country might mean the opposite (or something totally bizarre!) somewhere else. Check it out:

Body language	Country	What it means
Putting your thumb and index finger together to form an "o"	United States	"A" okay
	France	Zero, worthless
	Brazil	A major insult
Putting your index and middle finger into a "v"	United States	Victory or peace
	England	A rude challenge
Giving someone a thumbs up	United States	Good! Good going!
	Bangladesh	Buzz off!
	Japan	One
Curling your index finger toward someone	United States	Come here
	China	An insult
Twirling your finger around your head	United States	You're crazy! That's crazy!
	Argentina	You have a phone call

Body language	Country	What it means
Nodding your head up and down	United States	Yes
	Bulgaria, Turkey	No
Shaking your head side to side	United States	No
	Bulgaria, Turkey	Yes

HOW TO BE A GOOD LISTENER

Part of being a good conversationalist is being a great listener, because once you ask all those stimulating questions, you'll need to pay attention to the answers! Make a first impression that counts, and show someone you're fascinated by what they have to say, by making sure you:

1. **LOOK** at the person who's talking. You don't have to stare directly into his eyes the whole time (that might freak him out!), but try to keep your eyes on his face. Don't let your eyes wander around the room!

2. **LISTEN**, and try not to interrupt. There's nothing that'll frustrate people faster and make them want to move on to something else than being repeatedly cut off while they're making chit chat! Wait until the person finishes speaking before jumping in with something you want to say.

3. **ASK** questions to find out more. When there's a lull, come up with a good follow-up question like, "And *then* what happened?" or, "So, what did you think about that?"

4. **NOD** or say something to show you're interested, or that you understand. But don't overdo it—too much nodding can also look like you're impatiently waiting for the other person to finish up (or like your head is too heavy for your neck!).

5. **REPEAT** what you hear the speaker saying in your own words. This is a listening skill known as "mirroring." Basically, you *reflect* the person's feelings by saying something like "I see how that must've been surprising," or "So you were really blown away." It shows people that you're really listening and taking in what they're saying.

SO FAR YOU'VE TOLD ME THAT YOU'VE CLIMBED MOUNT EVEREST, SWAM ACROSS THE ATLANTIC, AND WALKED ACROSS THE SAHARA ... DID I MISS ANYTHING ?

Huh? What? Are you a good listener?

Decide for yourself! A good listener...

✔ Doesn't space out, but focuses on what the speaker is saying. If you catch yourself daydreaming while your friend Gabe tells you all about his family's road trip to the Grand Canyon, try to imagine what it must've felt like to have been there.

✔ Doesn't look bored when someone's telling you about the birds she saw on her hike through the woods, even if it *is* boring!

✔ Doesn't pretend to listen, tune someone out, and then try to cover it up by saying "mmm hmm." It might work for a while, but if your aunt is asking you what kind of vegetables she should plant in her garden and you're thinking about what you want to eat at your birthday party, you'll get caught! It's better to act like you're listening when you really *are*, or find a way to get out of the conversation, if you're not.

✔ Doesn't judge the person doing the talking. Maybe you think your friend is making a big deal out of nothing, or that the way he handled a situation didn't make sense. Try to put yourself in his shoes and understand the way he's feeling.

HOW TO SURVIVE A PARTY WHEN YOU DON'T KNOW ANYONE

Being stuck in a room full of strangers can be pretty intimidating. But you can take control and turn awkward moments into a chance to have fun, and maybe even make new friends! Just follow these tips (which also apply to the first day at camp, school, or any place where you don't know anyone!).

1. **Act confident** and hold your head up high. Remember, these folks don't know you—if you look and behave like you're a star, you might just fool someone! Who *wouldn't* want to hang out with you?

2. **Smile!** A smile shows that you're friendly—and makes you more approachable, no matter how good you already look.

3. **Get a drink or something to eat.** With something to sip and nibble on, you'll be less likely to fidget or play with your hands or hair—all signs that you're nervous.

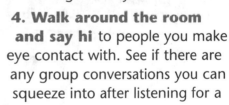

4. **Walk around the room and say hi** to people you make eye contact with. See if there are any group conversations you can squeeze into after listening for a few moments, or if anyone invites you into one.

5. **Find someone who's alone and strike up a conversation.** You don't have to say something brilliant—something basic like "What a great party! How do you know [the host]?" does the trick.

6. As a last resort, **look for the host** and ask him to introduce you to someone you might like, or offer to help out with refilling the munchies to keep yourself busy until it's time to leave.

HOW TO GET OUT OF A CONVERSATION THAT WON'T END

Your next-door neighbor loves to chat. You're all for being neighborly, but after the first five minutes, you've run out of things to say, and you aren't really interested in her going on and on and on and on about...what *is* she talking about anyway? You're not even listening anymore! You're fidgeting, inching your way toward the sidewalk, looking at your watch, sending her every non-verbal signal you can think of that should tell her you're bored of the conversation—and she's *still* not taking the hint! What do you do?

You don't want to be obnoxious, and you don't think she'll buy it if you point to the sky, shout "look over there!" and run away, either. So the best thing to do is to simply, gently, interrupt her and say, "I'm sorry! I'd love to chat longer, but I've *really* got to go. See you later." And then walk away with a friendly wave. But what if you're not in a place where you can simply walk away? What do you do if you're stuck with someone boring at a party, in a long line, or on the bus? Try these lines:

✔ "If you don't mind, I'm going to look for my friend now (or read my book)."

BLAH BLAH BLAH BLAH AND THEN... BLAH BLAH BLAH

✔ "Sorry, I've got a headache. I'm just going to sit here quietly for a little while and see if that helps."

✔ "I'm going to get started on my homework now, so I'll talk to you later."

✔ "I'm hungry. I'm going to go look for a snack. See ya!"

✔ "I'm so tired right now that I can't even *see* straight. Let's chat later."

What to Say When You've Forgotten Someone's Name

This kid walks toward you, smiling, and acting like he knows you. You remember his face but not his name. John? James? Jason? You have *no* idea! Yikes! What should you do?

- **Don't make a run for it!** That won't get you anywhere, and you'll have an even harder time making up for a stunt like that later!

- **Think quickly.** Before he says anything to you, reintroduce yourself by saying "Hi, remember me? I'm..." Hopefully, he'll follow your lead and say his name, too.

- **Go undercover.** If he's already started talking to you like you know each other, make polite chit chat without saying any name at all, until you can break away and secretly ask someone else what in the world his name is!

- **Get back-up.** If another friend of yours comes up to you both, say "Hey guys, why don't you introduce yourselves?" Then pay attention, and when the person in question says his name, don't yell out "RIGHT! Adam. I *knew* it was Adam!"

- **'Fess up!** Just say something like "*Arghh!* Your name is right on the tip of my tongue..." or, "Of course I know your name, but I'm blanking on it right now!" and let him help you. Then be extra friendly to make up for your forgetfulness!

THAT'S A MOUTHFUL! WHAT TO SAY WHEN YOU CAN'T PRONOUNCE A NAME

What if your problem isn't *remembering* someone's name, but getting it to roll off your tongue? No matter how hard you try, you just can't manage to get your new science partner Sean's name right the first time, second time—or ever. (Is his name pronounced "Seen" or "Shawn"?) What do you do?

a. Mumble his name under your breath whenever you have to say it, so that it sounds like something close enough.

b. Avoid using his name at all—just say, "hey, *there*!" or refer to him as "dude", "buddy", or "pal".

c. Give him a nickname that's close enough.

d. Apologize for your twisted tongue, and ask him to help you.

It's a little embarassing, but **d** is your best bet here. Even though you might get away with the first couple of options for a while, you can't keep it up forever! Besides, a person's name is something important, so you should try your best to get it right. One way is to ask your friend directly for tips on how to say his name correctly. Get him to write it out the way you pronounce it (like "shaw" for Xia) so that you can practice it, and then tell him to correct you when you get it wrong. If he offers you a shortened name or nickname, use it, but don't just make one up for him yourself!

How to make sure you don't forget another name!

1. **When someone says a name, listen to it carefully.** Sounds obvious? Well, sometimes you can be so busy noticing someone's shirt, trying *not* to notice his weird hair, or thinking of something clever to say next, that you don't actually pay attention. So the name goes in one ear and out the other!

2. **Repeat the name right away.** Say, "It's nice to meet you, Casey" and use the name again at the end of the conversation. At first, you may feel dorky doing this, but mentioning her name actually makes that person feel special (in addition to helping you remember it!).

3. **Try some of these tricks** to remember someone's name:

    a. **Think of someone else you know with the same name** and match it to the new person. If the name is Bart, think of Bart Simpson, or if the name is Jordan, think of Michael Jordan.

    b. **Come up with a word or phrase that rhymes with the name**, or sounds like it, like "Marge" and "barge", or "Eileen" and "I lean."

    c. **Choose a feature or personality trait of the person and link it to the name**, like Loud Laura or Happy Harry. It can be as silly as you want, if that helps you remember it, since the person never needs to know what it is!

    d. When you get home after meeting new people, **write their names down** in a notebook, and maybe also include the date, place, and occasion. That'll help to seal them in your memory.

That's NOT me! What to say to someone who always gets your name wrong

You've told her once. You've told her again. But it's been three months and one of your car pool moms is *still* calling you "ON-dree-a" instead of "AND-ree-a". It's making you crazy, especially because you *know* she must hear everyone *else* say your name the correct way. But you don't know how to bring it up after all this time without embarrassing her. What should you do?

a. Start saying her name wrong, too.

b. Ignore her whenever she calls your name and then say "What? Oh, I didn't *know* you were talking to *me*!"

c. Get your mom to say something about it to her.

d. Say, "I should have said something a long time ago, but my name is actually pronounced "AND-ree-a".

If you answered **d**, good going! The key is to be friendly and casual when you say it.

What to Say When You've Been Insulted

I'D LOVE TO PLAY TENNIS, BUT NOT WITH YOU

Isn't it the worst when somebody says something nasty to you out of the blue? And if that's not bad enough, you're so shocked by the words that you have absolutely no idea how to respond. So what *should* you say?

If the person didn't realize what he was saying, and didn't mean any offense, don't take any. Say something like, "I don't think you meant to say that."

If the person *meant* to be hurtful, it's a little rougher, but you can still recover and say something, instead of just fuming (and then thinking of all the things you *could* have said later!). Try not to get emotional or say something awful in return. Instead, be casual, and say something like, "I can't believe you just said that," or "I really take offense at your comment." Another approach is to say something like: "You can't win them all" or "And your point is?" if you can't think of a snappier comeback.

WAY TO GO!

What to Say When You've Been Complimented

Do you remember the last time someone said something really nice about you? It probably felt pretty great, right? Do you remember what you said in reply? Well, as weird as it sounds, many people feel uncomfortable accepting compliments and aren't sure what to say. Try the quiz on the next page to see how you handle it!

1. You're wearing your new shirt to school and see a friend. She tells you, "I love your shirt." Do you say:

  a. "*This?* It's laundry day and I found it at the bottom of my closet."

  b. "Thanks, I like it too."

  c. "Thanks, but I think I look weird in it."

  d. "Do you want it?"

2. You've just played the tuba at your school recital and your cousin comes up to you and says, "You played great!" Do you say:

  a. "I forgot my cues and was totally off key."

  b. "I'm glad you came to hear me play, thanks."

  c. "Jacob was playing better than me. You probably heard him."

  d. "I hate the tuba. My parents make me play it."

3. You've just played the soccer game of your life, and scored three goals. The losing team's goalie shakes your hand and says, "You played a great game." Do you say:

  a. "Thanks, but I think you were just off today."

  b. "Thanks, you guys put up a good fight."

  c. "Thanks, but I can't believe I missed that fourth goal!"

  d. "Thanks, you guys just need to practice more!"

4. Your friend comes up to you at a party and says, "You look great today." Do you say:

  a. "No, I don't!"

  b. "Thanks!"

  c. "Not as great as YOU!"

  d. "Isn't this jacket the best?"

If you answered anything other than **b** for all of the questions, then you need to work on taking a compliment! Maybe you don't realize it, but you tend to brush off the nice things people say to you. Why in the world would you do that? It could be that you're simply taken by surprise by their kind words and can't think of what to say. Or it could be that deep down you don't think that you really deserve the compliment. Or it could be that you don't want to seem like you're bragging. But whenever you receive a compliment, you *deserve* it, so enjoy the moment (and let the person who gave it feel good about it, too) by accepting it graciously.

How to take a compliment

- **Don't brag.** If someone says something nice about you, don't take that as an invitation to start rambling on and on about everything *else* that's great about you, too!

THANKS, NOT ONLY AM I GREAT AT SOCCER, BUT I'M ALSO A STRAIGHT A STUDENT, I EDIT THE SCHOOL NEWSPAPER, AND I RUN THREE MILES BEFORE BREAKFAST EVERY DAY!

- **Don't put yourself down.** When people appreciate something about you, don't try to convince them you really *don't* look good, that you really *didn't* do a great job, or that they really *don't* know what they're talking about.

- **Don't fish to give them a compliment in return.** If you can truly say, "I love your shirt, too!" then say it. But if you don't mean it, it'll be obvious that you're being phony, so it's better to just not say anything like that in return.

- **Be nice.** Say "thanks" as warmly as you can—it's really all the other person expects in return!

HOW TO GIVE THE BEST COMPLIMENTS EVER

- Make sure your praise is **sincere**. If you flatter people to make them feel better about themselves or just to get them to like you, they'll usually be able to see right through you (no x-ray goggles needed!).

- Be *specific* in your compliment. It'll make someone feel even better if you say, "That was a super presentation. You really knew your stuff and now I'm interested to learn more!" rather than saying something general like, "You're a good student."

- Try to compliment something that's *special* about somebody, or say something that he actually controls. It'll mean more if you say that you love the way your friend decorated his room, rather than complimenting him on the house he lives in (unless he built it himself!).

- Make sure that your compliment isn't mixed up with feelings of jealousy or criticism, and that it doesn't put anybody else down.

To give a genuine compliment:

Don't Say: "You play basketball so much better than Chris."

Do Say: "You play really well. I'm glad you joined our team."

Don't Say: "Congratulations on winning the spelling bee. I know I could've won with that word!"

Do Say: "Congratulations!"

Don't Say: "You look so much better than usual!"

Do Say: "You look great today."

Don't Say: "Nice shot! I was wondering when you were going to score."

Do Say: "Good shot!"

WHAT TO SAY WHEN YOU'RE ASKED TO SPEAK IN FRONT OF THE CLASS

So how *do* you get through those heart-stopping moments when you're called on to give a speech or a presentation?

HOW TO SPEAK UP AND BE HEARD

- **Take a deep breath** before starting to speak. If you're nervous, you might actually hold your breath without realizing it, and then find yourself gasping before you get to the end of your first sentence!

- **Find your natural voice** and speak with that. Most people's voices tend to get high and squeaky when they're nervous.

- **Don't make everything you say sound like a question**, which makes it seem like you're not very sure of what you're saying.

- **Vary your speed and volume**. Don't drone on and on and on in a monotone, or you'll lose your audience. It helps if you're really into the subject you're talking about.

SURVIVAL TIP!

Don't put yourself down for speaking your mind! The #1 way to sound confident and sure of yourself is to make sure you don't start off by *apologizing* for what you have to say! Don't say: "This is probably a stupid idea, but..." "I don't know why I'm saying this, but..." "I'm not very good at speaking in front of a group, but..."

WHAT TO SAY WHEN YOUR TEACHER IS WRONG

Even the best teachers make mistakes every now and then, right? What's the best way to correct them, without being a smart aleck?

- **If your teacher is doing a math problem on the board and makes an error**, there's nothing wrong with raising your hand and saying, "Mrs. Chalk, isn't 3 times 27 equal to 81, not 83?" Just make sure to be polite about it (that means no snickering!).

- **If your teacher is saying something that you're pretty sure isn't true** (like claiming that there's intelligent life on Mars), it's okay to challenge her. But it's a good idea to wait until the end of class to bring it up, instead of calling out "That's wrong!" in front of everyone. That way you're being respectful, and also, in case *you're* the one who ends up being mistaken, you won't make a fool out of yourself.

- **If your teacher makes an error correcting your paper or grading an exam**, you should definitely speak up. Do the math, check it twice, and be nice when you point out the mistake.

- **If your teacher wrongly blames you for something you didn't do**, you have every right to defend yourself. Calmly explain the situation and bring along any witnesses you can to back you up. It may not change the action your teacher takes this time (maybe you were already punished), but at least you stood up for yourself, and your teacher will remember that next time.

How to Speak Up For Someone Else

Someone says something nasty about someone else. You know it's not true. So what do you do?

Set the record straight.

It's as simple as that! It's important to share what you know, no matter if it's a teacher, a friend, your sworn enemy, or a total stranger saying bad stuff about someone. Use evidence, like your own personal experience, and remember to keep your cool (it doesn't do any good to defend someone else by acting like an idiot!).

Let's say you're with a group of friends and one of them says that the only reason the starting point guard on your basketball team scores so many points is because she plays dirty. You know that's simply not true—she plays hard, but never cheats. Just say, "That's not true. I play with her and I know that she plays by the rules." You'll feel better about yourself for having stood up for your teammate—and you'd want her to do the same for you, too!

HOW TO CONFRONT SOMEONE YOU THINK IS LYING

Is it possible to tell whether or not someone is lying to you just by the way he acts? Take this quiz to see if you can spot the liar!

TRUE OR FALSE: ARE YOU A LIE DETECTOR?

1. A person who is lying to you won't make eye contact with you and will look away instead.

True or False

2. A person who is lying will take a long time to answer your questions while thinking up stories.

True or False

3. A person who is lying will pause a lot while speaking and use a lot of "ums", "ahhs", and "you knows."

True or False

4. A person who is lying acts nervous, tapping his foot or fidgeting.

True or False

5. A person who is lying will laugh a lot or giggle more than normal.

True or False

6. A person who is lying will talk quickly and mumble words.

True or False

7. A person who is lying will slowly start to grow a longer nose.

True or False

ARE YOU **SURE** THAT'S WHAT HAPPENED?

8. You can never really know who is lying to you by their body language alone.

True or False

Are you ready to score your quiz? Well, the *only* true answer is that you can *never* know for sure if other people are lying to you, judging only by the way they act, or even by the things they say. Everyone has a different style of speaking (and nervous habits!), and if you thought all the quiz answers were true, you might end up thinking that a whole lot of completely innocent people were lying to you.

The only way to really know that someone is lying is if you have solid evidence, like witnessing an event that took place yourself, or having the say-so of someone who you trust completely. In those situations when you're confident that someone's not being honest, you might decide to confront the person. If you *do*, first try to think of the reasons why the person might be lying to you. Is it to cover up some kind of embarrassment, fear, or hurt? Then, think about the type of lie he told you. Was it a white lie, a lie of omission (that is, not telling you the whole story, or leaving out details), or a whopping big, awful lie of lies? Knowing the kind of lie should have an effect on your reaction.

If you decide to confront the person...

Don't Say:			Do Say:
Don't Say:	"I know that's not what happened!"	"Can we talk about..."	**Do Say:**
Don't Say:	"Tell me the truth!"	"Are you sure you've told me everything?"	**Do Say:**
Don't Say:	"You're a big liar!"	"I think you might be confused about what happened."	**Do Say:**
Don't Say:	"Joe will tell me what really happened!"	"I think we should talk to Joe, and see if he can help us sort out this misunderstanding."	**Do Say:**

WHAT TO SAY WHEN YOUR FRIEND'S PARENTS ARE SPLITTING UP

Your friend is crying and tells you that her parents are getting divorced. You don't know what you can say to make her feel better. What should you do?

- **Say that you're sorry to hear the news,** and that you know it must be really hard for her.

- **Tell her that,** no matter what happened between her folks, **it's not her fault.**

- **Offer to do whatever you can** to help her through, like having her come over and spend time with you at your home, or going out somewhere together.

- **Don't ask too many questions** about why her parents are splitting up, or anything too personal.

- **Ask about your friend's future** and what's going to happen next (like if she's going to move, or which parent she'll be living with).

- **Try to be positive.** Even if your friend is angry and says bad things about her parents, *don't* join in or agree with her (no matter *how* annoying you've always found her mom!).

- **If you've been through the same thing,** tell her that she'll be okay, just like you!

WHAT TO SAY WHEN YOUR FRIEND'S GRANDPA DIED

One of the hardest things in life is when someone you love dies. That's why when people you know lose someone important to them, it's hard to know what to say to comfort them. You might not feel comfortable saying anything at all the next time you see them, because you don't want to remind them of their loss, make them feel sad, or see them cry. But it's a good idea to say *something*, to let people know that you care, and to offer your support. Even if it doesn't seem like much, it'll mean a lot to them. So what *should* you say?

- **Say that you feel bad about their loss.** That doesn't mean you need to go on and on about how terribly sad you are, or how sad you think they must be—that could make them feel worse! Just say, "I'm really sorry to hear the news."

- **Ask if you can do anything for them.** Even if they say they're okay or don't need anything, try to think of a few things that might be helpful to do (like walking their dog, or helping them with homework, or anything else you can think of), and offer to do them.

- **Tell them that you're there.** Let them know that you're around if they need to talk, or want to do something to get their mind off of things for a while, like go for a walk.

- **Offer a memory.** If you know the person who died, it's always nice to have a few good words to say about that person.

- **Give your friend a hug.** Sometimes the best way to say you care isn't with words at all!

WHAT TO SAY WHEN YOUR BEST FRIEND IS MOVING AWAY

You can't believe it. Your best friend for the last six years is moving away. It's hard to imagine life without him, and you're dreading the day he drives off. But even though it'll be hard for you, you realize that it's going to be even worse for him to have to leave his home, friends, school, and everything he knows behind. What can you say to make him feel better about it?

- **Promise to keep in touch.** Remind him that nowadays, with e-mail, long-distance calling plans, and instant messaging, it's easier (and cheaper) than ever to talk to people on the other side of the country—and even the opposite side of the world!

- **Tell your friend that you're going to miss him,** and see if you can plan to visit each other during vacations.
- **Ask him about what his new neighborhood will be like,** and help him to find out what fun things there are to do around there.
- **Offer to help him pack up his room.**

HOW TO PUT WHAT YOU WANT TO SAY IN WRITING

Just because you've got something to say doesn't mean you have to actually open your mouth or utter even one little word! At times, it's much easier to pour out your feelings into a letter and pop it in the mail—or compose an e-mail and hit "send"—than to talk to someone face to face. Your pen or computer mouse can seem like a good choice when you're too sad, afraid, embarrassed, angry, sorry, or overwhelmed to talk to someone directly. But beware! Putting your thoughts down on paper, or displaying them on a screen, has its own dangers, so make sure you think it through before letting your fingers do the talking for you!

SURVIVAL TIP!
Put it away!

After you've poured out your deepest feelings and thoughts into a letter, put it away for a day or two before sending it. Then read it again, see if you still feel the same way, and decide if you really want to send it. If not, just tear it up or delete it, and no one will ever know!

You Did It!

Phew! **You've survived** a whole lot this month!

From being insulted, to getting a gift you hate, to confronting a friend who won't stop telling you what to do—you learned to deal with all kinds of embarrassing, humiliating, and awkward moments. You got lots of tips and tools for dealing with people—parents, teachers, siblings, friends, and even total strangers. You've learned to **say what you mean, mean what you say** and arm yourself with the right words, attitudes, and actions you need to survive anything, any time, anywhere!

So now your job is to take all that you've gained and remember it, practice it, and use it to **get what you want**. And if you ever find yourself facing any challenge that isn't covered in this book, you *can* get through it, if you remember to: be honest (or not!) when you need to, to stick up for yourself (or back off!) when you have to, and to trust yourself and respect others (always!). With those simple rules in mind, you'll be ready to survive anything!

OKAY, SO NOW I KNOW HOW TO SAY WHAT I MEAN, MEAN WHAT I SAY, AND GET WHAT I WANT!